MEDITATIONS
OF
JOHN
MUIR

Nature's
Temple

# MEDITATIONS
## OF
# JOHN
# MUIR

## Nature's Temple

*Compiled and edited by*
## CHRIS HIGHLAND

 WILDERNESS PRESS • BERKELEY

Copyright © 2001 Chris High

FIRST EDITION July 2001
**Second printing December 2001**

Book and cover design by Larry B. Van Dyke
Photographs by the author except where otherwise noted
Cover photos: *Portrait of John Muir* courtesy of the National
              Park Service; *Sequoia-Kings Canyon* and
              *Grandmother Tree* © 2001 Chris Highland
Frontispiece photo: *John Muir* courtesy of the National Park
              Service

Library of Congress Card Number 2001026326
ISBN 0-89997-285-3

Manufactured in the United States of America
Published by: **Wilderness Press**
              **1200 5th Street**
              **Berkeley, CA 94710**
              **(800) 443-7227; FAX (510) 558-1696**
              *mail@wildernesspress.com*
              **www.wildernesspress.com**

              Contact us for a free catalog

Printed on recycled paper, 20% post-consumer waste

**Library of Congress Cataloging-in-Publication Data**

Meditations of John Muir : nature's temple / compiled and edited by
Chris Highland.—
1st ed.
        p. cm.
    Includes bibliographical references (p. ).
    ISBN 0-89997-285-3
    1. Muir, John, 1838–1914.  2. Meditations.  I. Highland, Chris, 1955–

    QH31.M9 N34 2001
    508—dc21

                                        2001026326

# Introduction

*. . . as far as I can I must drift about these love-monument*
*mountains, glad to be a servant of servants*
*in so holy a wilderness.*

~John of the Mountains

On a recent return trip from Scotland, the land of
John Muir's birth, I met a young couple from
Glasgow who had never heard of their fellow
countryman. As they flew into California for the first
time, and newlyweds at that, I told them of Muir's
Scottish spirit alive in Muir Woods, Martinez, and
Sequoia, Kings Canyon, and Yosemite national parks.
The more I told them of the natural delights enjoyed
by Muir, the more thrilled they were to begin their
adventure. Fresh from my own pilgrimage to Muir's
birthplace in Dunbar, I felt a renewed kinship with
the man who said, "I care to live only to entice
people to look at Nature's loveliness."

John Muir (1838-1914) made enticement a
spiritual quality. His enthusiastic preaching of the
natural world sprang directly from his joyful
immersion in the soul of it all. In my journal from
that second journey across the sea I wrote, "The
thought is constant—go to the church of Nature. Let
the tired and worn out go. Go! Drop it and Go! Go
to the beauty of life that is free and open to
everyone. Go and just be there in it, as a part of it.

Fly with the geese, thunder with the falls of the Clyde [river], scootch up the castle ruins, graze with the woolly sheep . . . Breathe Life deeply. Live!"

This is the effect Muir can have on you if you are not careful! You venture out into the wilds where you have to depend on your intuition, on Nature's way, on your deeper sense of belonging. What some call faith or spirituality is that risking, that longing and belonging. Muir knew it, felt it, lived it.

As a patriarch of the American environmental movement, Muir engendered many conservation and ecological families. He helped to give birth to the national park system, the Sierra Club, and a myriad of smaller groups devoted to saving rivers, redwoods, and wildlife. Yet, he is also a spiritual parent who leads us down unmarked trails of the spirit. By urging us to simply be present in the world around us, loving and honoring it as our garden home, his poetic insight liberates life.

Every spiritual lesson we need is subtly and spectacularly evident in Nature. I have gleaned this insight from years of hiking the world's wisdom traditions. But mostly I have learned it in Muir's teeming forest. He teaches that we can step out beyond the books, the traditions, the philosophies that restrict the free rivering of our minds and dam the creativity of our communities; we may follow our streams into forests yet to be found. To climb with Muir is to reach remarkable vistas where we can see the smallest and the grandest as one forest — as one interwoven whole. At the end of each trail is a celebration of this organic unity, a bow and a dance of reverence and joy.

The readings in this book represent only a small portion of Muir's thought. To call them "meditations" is a bit presumptuous. Yet I believe he would be pleased and honored to know that readers

turn to his scribblings for inspiration and guidance, not merely to study them for their historical, scientific, or tourist data. He would find what he called 'inexpressible delight' in the companionship of the spiritual teachers, poets, and philosophers who join him on these pages. To us all he says there are higher lands of the mind, of the heart.

Invite Muir to help you jump the boulders into yourself. Allow him to guide your way like an expert tracker to what Thoreau called the Art of God, what Gautama Buddha called Awakening, and Jesus called the Home of God. His words can point you to what the Hindu peoples have called Atman, Jews address as Adonai, Emerson termed the Oversoul, and Muslims worship as Allah.

Let John Muir lead you along the ultimate adventure that treks every range of light. Then venture off on your own deertrails of the heart, harkening to his granite gospel that calls for you "to get as near to the heart of the world" as you can. Going out or going in, the cathedral doors are wide open!

Chris Highland,
Summer 2001

*Go now and then for fresh life—*
*if most of humanity must go through this*
*town stage of development—*
*just as divers hold their breath and come ever and anon*
*to the surface to breathe. . . .*
*Go whether or not you have faith. . . .*
*Form parties, if you must be social,*
*to go to the snow-flowers in winter,*
*to the sun-flowers in summer. . . .*
*Anyway, go up and away for life;*
*be fleet!*

~John of the Mountains

# Contents

In Memory Of

# JOHN LEES

*Whose homeland was Scotland
and
Who died homeless in America*

,

# 1

## God's First Temples

A few minutes ago every tree was excited, bowing to the roaring storm, waving, swirling, tossing their branches in glorious enthusiasm like worship. But though to the outer ear these trees are now silent, their songs never cease. Every hidden cell is throbbing with music and life, every fibre thrilling like harp strings, while incense is ever flowing from the balsam bells and leaves. No wonder the hills and groves were God's first temples, and the more they are cut down and hewn into cathedrals and churches, the farther off and dimmer seems the Lord.

The same may be said of stone temples. Yonder, to the eastward of our camp grove, stands one of Nature's cathedrals, hewn from the living rock, almost conventional in form, about two thousand feet high, nobly adorned with spires and pinnacles, thrilling under floods of sunshine as if alive like a grove-temple, and well named "Cathedral Peak."

"*The God dwelling in the temple of the body at last becomes the temple itself.*"

~Vivekananda

# 2

## Home to the Mountains

To the timid traveler, fresh from the sedimentary levels of the lowlands, these highways, however picturesque and grand, seem terribly forbidding—cold, dead, gloomy gashes in the bones of the mountains, and of all Nature's ways the ones to be most cautiously avoided. Yet they are full of the finest and most telling examples of Nature's love; and though hard to travel, none are safer. . . . True, there are innumerable places where the careless step will be the last step; and a rock falling from the cliffs may crush without warning like lightning from the sky; but what then? Accidents in the mountains are less common than in the lowlands, and these mountain mansions are decent, delightful, even divine, places to die in, compared with the doleful chambers of civilization. Few places in this world are more dangerous than home. Fear not, therefore, to try the mountain-passes. They will kill care, save you from deadly apathy, set you free, and call forth every faculty into vigorous, enthusiastic action. Even the sick should try these so-called dangerous passes, because for every unfortunate they kill, they cure a thousand.

*"For the Home of God is at hand!"*
~Jesus of Nazareth

# 3

## To Gain a Perfect View

I was eager to reach the extreme verge [of Yosemite Creek] to see how it behaved in flying so far through the air; but after enjoying this view and getting safely away I have never advised any one to follow my steps. The last incline down which the stream journeys so gracefully is so steep and smooth one must slip cautiously forward on hands and feet alongside the rushing water, which so near one's head is very exciting. But to gain a perfect view one must go yet farther, over a curving brow to a slight shelf on the extreme brink. . . . To me it seemed nerve-trying to slip to this narrow foothold and poise on the edge of such a precipice so close to the confusing whirl of the waters. . . . So glorious a display of pure wildness, acting at close range while cut off from all the world beside, is terribly impressive. . .the rainbow light forming one of the most glorious pictures conceivable.

*"In Wildness is the preservation of the World."*
~Henry Thoreau

# 4

## This Living Ceiling

Though the commonest and most widely distributed of all the ferns, I might almost say that I never saw it before. The broad-shouldered fronds held high on smooth stout stalks growing close together, overleaning and overlapping, make a complete ceiling, beneath which one may walk erect over several acres without being seen, as if beneath a roof. And how soft and lovely the light streaming through this living ceiling, revealing the arching branching ribs and veins of the fronds as the framework of countless panes of pale green and yellow plant-glass nicely fitted together—a fairyland created out of the commonest fern-stuff. . . . I sat a long time beneath the tallest fronds, and never enjoyed anything in the way of a bower of wild leaves more strangely impressive. Only spread a fern frond over your head and worldly cares are cast out, and freedom and beauty and peace come in. The waving of a pine tree on the top of a mountain—a magic wand in Nature's hand—every devout mountaineer knows its power; but the marvelous beauty value of what the Scotch call a breckan in a still dell, what poet has sung this?

*"The one who meditates on the Divine is like a tree planted by streams of water."*

~Psalm 1

# 5

## Everything Is Flowing

Contemplating the lace-like fabric of streams outspread over the mountains, we are reminded that everything is flowing—going somewhere, animals and so-called lifeless rocks as well as water. Thus the snow flows fast or slow in grand beauty-making glaciers and avalanches; the air in majestic floods carrying minerals, plant leaves, seeds, spores, with streams of music and fragrance; water streams carrying rocks both in solution and in the form of mud particles, sand, pebbles, and boulders. Rocks flow from volcanoes like water from springs, and animals flock together and flow in currents modified by stepping, leaping, gliding, flying, swimming, etc. While the stars go streaming through space pulsed on and on forever like blood globules in Nature's warm heart.

*"Throb thine with Nature's throbbing breast."*
~Ralph Waldo Emerson

6

# A Temple Lighted From Above

The most famous and accessible of these canyon valleys, and also the one that presents their most striking and sublime features on the grandest scale, is the Yosemite, situated in the basin of the Merced River at an elevation of 4000 feet above the level of the sea. It is about seven miles long, half a mile to a mile wide, and nearly a mile deep in the solid granite flank of the range. The walls are made up of rocks, mountains in size, partly separated from each other by side canyons, and they are so sheer in front, and so compactly and harmoniously arranged on a level floor, that the Valley, comprehensively seen; looks like an immense hall or temple lighted from above.

But no temple made with hands can compare with Yosemite. Every rock in its walls seems to glow with life. Down through the middle of the Valley flows the crystal Merced, River of Mercy, peacefully quiet, reflecting lilies and trees and the onlooking rocks; things frail and fleeting and types of endurance meeting here and blending in countless forms as if into this one mountain mansion Nature had gathered her choicest treasures, to draw her lovers into close and confiding communion with her.

*"Make haste, my beloved,*
*and be like a young stag upon the mountains."*
~Song of Songs

# 7

AltarFalls

One of these ancient flood boulders stands firm in the middle of the stream channel. . . . It is a nearly cubical mass of granite about eight feet high, plushed with mosses over the top and down the sides to ordinary high-water mark. When I climbed on top of it today and lay down to rest, it seemed the most romantic spot I had yet found—the one big stone with its mossy level top and smooth sides standing square and firm and solitary, like an altar, the fall in front of it bathing it lightly with the finest of the spray, just enough to keep its moss cover fresh; the clear green pool beneath, with its foam-bells and its half circle of lilies leaning forward like a band of admirers, and flowering dogwood and alder trees leaning over all in sun-sifted arches. How soothingly, restfully cool it is beneath that leafy, translucent ceiling, and how delightful the water music—the deep bass tones of the fall, the clashing, ringing spray, and infinite variety of small low tones of the current gliding past the side of the boulder-island, and glinting against a thousand smaller stones down the ferny channel! All this shut in; every one of these influences acting at short range as if in a quiet room. The place seemed holy, where one might hope to see God.

*"The world is a sacred vessel."*
~The Tao Te Ching

# 8

## The Face of God

This has been by far the most beautiful and gentle of our Arctic days, the water perfectly glassy and with no swell, mirroring the sky, which shows a few blue cloudless spots, white as satin near the horizon, of beautiful luster, trying to the eyes. Gulls skimming the glassy level. Innumerable multitudes of eider ducks, the snowy shore, and all the highest mountains cloud-capped—a rare picture and perfectly tranquil and peaceful! God's love is manifest in the landscape as in a face. How unlike yesterday! In the evening a long approach to sunset, a red sky mingling with brown and white of the ice-blink. Growing colder towards midnight. There is no night at all now; only a partial gloaming; never, even in cloudy midnights, too dark to read.

*"Love is the strongest force the world possesses."*
~Mahatma Gandhi

# 9

## Every Day a Holiday

When I set out on the long excursion that finally led to California I wandered afoot and alone, from Indiana to the Gulf of Mexico, with a plant-press on my back, holding a generally southward course, like the birds when they are going from summer to winter. From the west coast of Florida I crossed the gulf to Cuba, enjoyed the rich tropical flora there for a few months, intending to go thence to the north end of South America, make my way through the woods to the headwaters of the Amazon, and float down that grand river to the ocean. But I was unable to find a ship bound for South America—fortunately perhaps, for I had incredibly little money for so long a trip and had not yet fully recovered from a fever caught in the Florida swamps. Therefore I decided to visit California for a year or two to see its wonderful flora and the famous Yosemite Valley. All the world was before me and every day was a holiday, so it did not seem important to which one of the world's wildernesses I first should wander.

*"Homeless I wander, in company with God."*
~Basho

# 10

## A Hopeless Task

Nowhere will you see the majestic operations of Nature more clearly revealed beside the frailest, most gentle and peaceful things. Nearly all the park is a profound solitude. Yet it is full of charming company, full of God's thoughts, a place of peace and safety amid the most exalted grandeur and eager enthusiastic action, a new song, a place of beginnings abounding in first lessons of life, mountain-building, eternal, invincible, unbreakable order; with sermons in stones, storms, trees, flowers, and animals brimful of humanity. . . .

But to get all this into words is a hopeless task. The leanest sketch of each feature would need a whole chapter. Nor would any amount of space, however industriously scribbled, be of much avail. To defrauded town toilers, parks in magazine articles are like pictures of bread to the hungry. I can write only hints to incite good wanderers to come to the feast.

*"To rarely speak—such is the way of Nature."*
~The Tao Te Ching

# 11

## The Glorious Festival

A nd the winds, too, were singing in wild accord, playing on every tree and rock, surging against the huge brows and domes and outstanding battlements, deflected hither and thither and broken into a thousand cascading, roaring currents in the canyons, and low bass, drumming swirls in the hollows. . . . This was the most sublime waterfall flood I ever saw—clouds, winds, rocks, waters, throbbing together as one. And then to contemplate what was going on simultaneously with all this in other mountain temples; the Big Tuolumne Canyon—how the white waters and the winds were singing there! And in Hetch Hetchy Valley and the great King's River yosemite, and in all the other Sierra canyons, and valleys from Shasta to the southernmost fountains of the Kern, thousands of rejoicing flood waterfalls chanting together in jubilee dress.

*"Words are like the wind and the waves. . .*
*flow with whatever may happen and let your mind be free;*
*stay centered."*

~Chuang Tzu

# 12

## There Were Giants

During my first years in the Sierra I was ever calling on everybody within reach to admire them, but I found no one half warm enough until Emerson came. I had read his essays, and felt sure that of all men he would best interpret the sayings of these noble mountains and trees. Nor was my faith weakened when I met him in Yosemite. He seemed as serene as a sequoia. . . . I said to him, "The mountains are calling; run away, and let plans and parties and dragging lowland duties all 'gang tapsal-teerie.' We'll go up a canyon singing your own song, 'Good-bye, proud world! I'm going home!' Up there lies a new heaven and a new earth." But alas, it was too late—it was too near the sundown of his life.

Accustomed to reach whatever place I started for, I was going up the mountain alone to camp, and wait the coming of the party next day. But since Emerson was so soon to vanish, I concluded to stop with him. He hardly spoke a word all the evening, yet it was a great pleasure simply to be near him, warming in the light of his face as at a fire. In the morning we walked through a fine group [of sequoias], he said "There were giants in those days." Later I urged him to stay. "You are yourself a sequoia." But he waved me a last good-bye. [Seventeen years later] I stood beside his grave. He had gone to higher Sierras, and, as I fancied, was again waving his hand in friendly recognition.

"The root of all is planted in you."
~Bauls of Bengal

# 13

## Bathed in Beauty

The forests, too, seem kindly familiar, and the lakes and meadows and glad singing streams. I should like to dwell with them forever. Here with bread and water I should be content. Even if not allowed to roam and climb, tethered to a stake or tree in some meadow or grove, even then I should be content forever. Bathed in such beauty, watching the expressions ever varying on the faces of the mountains, watching the stars, which here have a glory that the lowlander never dreams of, watching the circling seasons, listening to the songs of the waters and winds and birds, would be endless pleasure. And what glorious cloudlands I should see, storms and calms—a new heaven and a new earth every day, aye and new inhabitants. And how many visitors I should have. I feel sure I should not have one dull moment. And why should this appear extravagant? It is only common sense, a sign of health, genuine, natural, all-awake health. One would be at an endless Godful play, and what speeches and music and acting and scenery and lights!—sun, moon, stars, auroras. Creation just beginning, the morning stars "still singing together and all the children of God shouting for joy."

*"To touch a snowflake, to feed [the deer], was to touch them all."*

~Helen Hoover

# 14

## To Guide My Humbled Body

After I had passed the tall groves that stretch a mile above Mirror Lake, and scrambled around the Tenaya Fall, which is just at the head of the lake groves, I crept through the dense and spiny chaparral that plushes the roots of the mountains here for miles in warm green, and was ascending a precipitous rock-front, smoothed by glacial action, when I suddenly fell—for the first time since I touched foot to Sierra rocks. After several somersaults, I became insensible from the shock, and when consciousness returned I found myself wedged among short, stiff bushes, trembling as if cold, not injured in the slightest. Judging by the sun, I could not have been insensible very long; probably not a minute, possibly an hour; and I could not remember what made me fall, or where I had fallen from; but I saw that if I had rolled a little further, my mountain-climbing would have been finished. I had not yet reached the most difficult portion of the canyon, but I determined to guide my humbled body over the most nerve-trying places I could find; for I was now awake, and felt confident that the last of the town fog had been shaken from both head and feet.

*"Did Allah not find you an orphan and give you shelter?*
*Did Allah not guide you?"*

~The Qur'an

# 15

## Spiritual Flight

When the avalanche started I threw myself on my back and spread my arms to try to keep from sinking. Fortunately, though the grade of the canyon is very steep, it is not interrupted by precipices large enough to cause outbounding or free plunging. On no part of the rush was I buried. I was only moderately embedded on the surface or at times a little below it, and covered with a veil of back-streaming dust particles; and as the whole mass beneath and about me joined in the flight there was no friction, though I was tossed here and there and lurched from side to side. When the avalanche swedged and came to rest I found myself on top of the crumpled pile without a bruise or scar. This was a fine experience. . . . This flight in what might be called a milky way of snow-stars was the most spiritual and exhilarating of all the modes of motion I have ever experienced. Elijah's flight in a chariot of fire could hardly have been more gloriously exciting.

"[And after the wind, the avalanche, the earthquake, the fire]
a sound of sheer silence."

~Elijah

# 16

## Nature's Bible

The main object of the missionaries was to ascertain the spiritual wants of the warlike Chilcat tribe. . .while my mind was on the mountains, glaciers and forests. . . . Cares of every kind were quickly forgotten, and though the [river steamer] Cassiar engines began to wheeze and sigh with doleful solemnity, suggesting coming trouble, we were too happy to mind them. Every face glowed with natural love of wild beauty. The islands were seen in long perspective, their forests dark green in the foreground, with varying tones of blue growing more and more tender in the distance; bays full of hazy shadows, graduating into open, silvery fields of light, and lofty headlands with fine arching insteps dipping their feet in the shining water. But every eye was turned to the mountains. Forgotten now were the Chilcats and missions while the word of God was being read in these majestic hieroglyphics blazoned along the sky. The earnest, childish wonderment with which this glorious page of Nature's Bible was contemplated was delightful to see. All evinced eager desire to learn.

*"The books the Holy Spirit is writing are living."*
~Father Jean-Pierre DeCaussade

# 17

## Eyes To See, Ears To Hear

It seems strange that visitors to Yosemite should be so little influenced by its novel grandeur, as if their eyes were bandaged and their ears stopped. Most of those I saw yesterday were looking down as if wholly unconscious of anything going on about them, while the sublime rocks were trembling with the tones of the mighty chanting congregation of waters gathered from all the mountains round about, making music that might draw angels out of heaven. Yet respectable-looking, even wise-looking people were fixing bits of worms on bent pieces of wire to catch trout. Sport they called it. Should church-goers try to pass the time fishing in baptismal fonts while dull sermons were being preached, the so-called sport might not be so bad; but to play in the Yosemite temple, seeking pleasure in the pain of fishes struggling for their lives, while God is preaching the sublimest water and stone sermons!

*"Then the angel showed me the river of the water of life, flowing from [the Creator]. . . on either side. . . the tree of life."*
~John of Patmos

# 18

## All the Air Is Music

The water ouzel, in his rocky home amid foaming waters. How romantic and beautiful is the life of this brave little singer on the wild mountain streams, building his round bossy nest of moss by the side of a rapid or fall, where it is sprinkled and kept fresh and green by the spray! No wonder he sings well, since all the air about him is music; every breath he draws is part of a song, and he gets his first music lessons before he is born; for the eggs vibrate in time with the tones of the waterfalls. Bird and stream are inseparable, songful and wild, gentle and strong—the bird ever in danger in the midst of the stream's mad whirlpools, yet seemingly immortal. And so I might go on, writing words, words, words; but to what purpose? Go see him and love him, and through him as through a window look into Nature's warm heart.

*"We have fallen into the place where everything is music."*
~Rumi

# 19

## The Shaking Temple

At half-past two o'clock of a moonlit morning in March, I was awakened by a tremendous earthquake, and though I had never before enjoyed a storm of this sort, the strange thrilling motion could not be mistaken, and I ran out of my cabin, both glad and frightened, shouting, "A noble earthquake!" . . . as if Nature were wrecking her Yosemite temple, and getting ready to build a still better one.

[To calm one visitor's fears] I said, "Come, cheer up; smile a little and clap your hands, now that kind Mother Earth is trotting us on her knee to amuse us and make us good." In this work of beauty, every boulder is prepared and measured and put in its place more thoughtfully than are the stones of temples. If for a moment you are inclined to regard these taluses as mere draggled, chaotic dumps, climb to the top of one of them, and run down without any haggling, puttering hesitation, boldly jumping from boulder to boulder with even speed. You will then find your feet playing a tune, and quickly discover the music and poetry of these magnificent rock piles—a fine lesson; and all Nature's wildness tells the same story—the shocks and outbursts of earthquakes, volcanoes, geysers, roaring, thundering waves and floods, the silent uprush or sap in plants, storms of every sort—each and all are the orderly beauty-making love-beats of Nature's heart.

*"Even heaven and the highest heaven cannot contain You, how much less this house that I have built!"*

~Solomon

# 20

## Of All Places the Best

Steaming solemnly out of the fjord and down the coast, the islands and mountains were again passed in review; the clouds that so often hide the mountaintops even in good weather were now floating high above them, and the transparent shadows they cast were scarce perceptible on the white glacier fountains. So abundant and novel are the objects of interest in a pure wilderness that unless you are pursuing special studies it matters little where you go, or how often to the same place. Wherever you chance to be always seems at the moment of all places the best; and you feel that there can be no happiness in this world or in any other for those who may not be happy here.

*"When the clouds rise,*
*Ndjambi's [God's] voice is clearly heard."*

~African Bantu

# 21
## Life Before Death

We find in the fields of Nature no place that is blank or barren; every spot on land or sea is covered with harvests, and these harvests are always ripe and ready to be gathered, and no toiler is ever underpaid. Not in these fields, God's wilds, will you ever hear the sad moan of disappointment, 'All is vanity.' No, we are overpaid a thousand times for all our toil, and a single day in so divine an atmosphere of beauty and love would be well worth living for, and at its close, should death come, without any hope of another life, we could still say, "Thank you, God, for the glorious gift!" and pass on. Indeed, some of the days I have spent alone in the depths of the wilderness have shown me that immortal life beyond the grave is not essential to perfect happiness, for these diverse days were so complete there was no sense of time in them, they had no definite beginning or ending, and formed a kind of terrestrial immortality. After days like these we are ready for any fate—pain, grief, death or oblivion— with grateful heart for the glorious gift as long as hearts shall endure. In the meantime, our indebtedness is growing ever more. The sun shines and the stars, and new beauty meets us at every step in all our wanderings.

*"The Sun Goddess was in her sacred weaving hall,*
*weaving garments of the Gods."*

~Shinto

# 22

## Fellow Wanderer

The waycup, or flicker, so familiar to every [child] in the old Middle West States, is one of the most common of the wood-peckers hereabouts, and makes one feel at home. I can see no difference in plumage or habits from the Eastern species, though the climate here is so different—a fine, brave, confiding, beautiful bird. The robin, too, is here, with all his familiar notes and gestures, tripping daintily on open garden spots and high meadows. Over all America he seems to be at home, moving from the plains to the mountains and from north to south, back and forth, up and down, with the march of the seasons and food supply. How admirable the constitution and temper of this brave singer, keeping in cheery health over so vast and varied a range! Oftentimes, as I wander through these solemn woods, awe-striken and silent, I hear the reassuring voice of this fellow wanderer ringing out, sweet and clear, "Fear not! Fear not!"

*"Split a piece of wood, and I am there.*
*Pick up a stone, and you will find me there."*
~Gospel of Thomas

# 23

## Sky Flowers

Contemplating the works of these flowers of the sky, one may easily fancy them endowed with life: messengers sent down to work in the mountain mines on errands of divine love. Silently flying through the darkened air, swirling, glinting, to their appointed places, they seem to have taken counsel together, saying, "Come, we are feeble; let us help one another. We are many, and together we will be strong. Marching in close, deep ranks, let us roll away the stones from these mountain sepulchers, and set the landscapes free. Let us uncover these clustering domes. Here let us carve a lake basin; there, a Yosemite Valley; here, a channel for a river with fluted steps and brows for the plunge of songful cataracts. Yonder let us spread broad sheets of soil, that human and beast may be fed; and here pile trains of boulders for pines and giant Sequoias. Here make ground for a meadow; there, for a garden and grove, making it smooth and fine for small daisies and violets and beds of heathy bryanthus, spicing it well with crystals, garnet feldspar, and zircon." Thus and so on it has oftentimes seemed to me sang and planned and labored the hearty snow-flower crusaders; and nothing that I can write can possibly exaggerate the grandeur and beauty of their work.

*"I wish to say nothing. What does the sky say?"*
~Confucius

# 24

## The Very Best Bed Imaginable

It is from this tree, called Red Fir by the lumber-men, that mountaineers cut boughs to sleep on when they are so fortunate as to be within its limit. Two or three rows of the sumptuous plushy-fronded branches, overlapping along the middle, and a crescent of smaller plumes mixed to one's taste with ferns and flowers for a pillow, form the very best bed imaginable. The essence of the pressed leaves seems to fill every pore of one's body. Falling water makes a soothing hush, while the spaces between the grand spires afford noble openings through which to gaze dreamily into the starry sky. The fir woods are fine sauntering-grounds at almost any time of year, but finest in autumn when the noble trees are hushed in the hazy light and drip with balsam; and the flying, whirling seeds, escaping from the ripe cones, mottle the air like flocks of butterflies. Even in the richest part of these unrivaled forests where so many noble trees challenge admiration we linger fondly among the colossal firs and extol their beauty again and again, as if no other tree in the world could henceforth claim our love.

*"I am never alone in this wild forest, this forest of elders, this forest of eyes."*
~Richard Nelson

# 25

## Only a Part

The world, we are told, was made especially for
humans—a presumption not supported by all the
facts. . .Why should humanity value itself as more
than a small part of the one great unit of creation?
And what creature of all that the Lord has taken the
pains to make is not essential to the completeness of
that unit—the cosmos? The universe would be
incomplete without humans; but it would also be
incomplete without the smallest transmicroscopic
creature that dwells beyond our conceitful eyes and
knowledge. From the dust of the earth, from the
common elementary fund, the Creator has made
Homo Sapiens. From the same material God has
made every other creature, however noxious and
insignificant to us. They are earth-born companions
and our fellow mortals.

*"And I saw that the sacred hoop of my people*
*was one of many hoops that made one circle."*
~Black Elk

# 26

## On and On into Infinite Mystery

Probably these gallflies make mistakes at times, like anybody else; but when they do, there is simply a failure of that particular brood, while enough to perpetuate the species do find the proper plants and nourishment. Many mistakes of this kind might be made without being discovered by us. Once a pair of wrens made the mistake of building a nest in the sleeve of a workman's coat, which was called for at sundown, much to the consternation and discomfiture of the birds. Still the marvel remains that any of the children of such small people as gnats and mosquitoes should escape their own and their parents' mistakes, as well as the vicissitudes of the weather and hosts of enemies, and come forth in full vigor and perfection to enjoy the sunny world. When we think of the small creatures that are visible, we are led to think of many that are smaller still and lead us on and on into infinite mystery.

*"The inner—what is it? if not intensified sky;*
*hurled through with birds and deep with the winds*
*of homecoming."*
~Rainer Maria Rilke

# 27

## Climbing Out of Hell

One of our best playgrounds was the famous old Dunbar Castle to which King Edward fled after his defeat at Bannockburn. It was built more than a thousand years ago, and though we knew little of its history, we had heard many mysterious stories of the battles fought about its walls, and firmly believed that every bone we found in the ruins belonged to an ancient warrior. We tried to see who could climb highest on the crumbling peaks and crags, and took chances that no cautious mountaineer would try. That I did not fall and finish my rock-scrambling in those adventurous boyhood days seems now a reasonable wonder. . . .

I was so proud of my skill as a climber that when I first heard of hell from a servant girl who loved to tell its horrors and warn us that if we did anything wrong we would be cast into it, I always insisted that I could climb out of it. I imagined it was only a sooty pit with stone walls like those of the castle, and I felt sure there must be chinks and cracks in the masonry for fingers and toes. Anyhow the terrors of the horrible place seldom lasted long beyond the telling; for natural faith casts out fear.

*"Whoever knows me can never fall—For I am love, which the vast expanse of evil can never still."*

~Hildegard of Bingen

# 28

## They Would Live Forever

The Juniper or Red Cedar is preeminently a rock tree, occupying the baldest domes and pavements in the upper silver fir and alpine zones, at a height of from 7000 to 9500 feet. Some trees are mere storm-beaten stumps about as broad as long, decorated with a few leafy sprays, reminding one of the crumbling towers of old castles scantily draped with ivy. . . . Most of the trees eight or ten feet thick, standing on pavements, are more than twenty centuries old rather than less. Barring accidents, for all I can see they would live forever; even when overthrown by avalanches, they refuse to lie at rest, lean stubbornly on their big branches as if anxious to rise, and while a single root holds to the rock, put forth fresh leaves with a grim, never-say-die expression.

*"Such a path could only be travelled by one. . . sensitive to the landmarks of a trackless wilderness."*
~Thomas Merton

# 29

## Possessed of a New Sense

After attaining an elevation of about 12,800 feet, I found myself at the foot of a sheer drop in the bed of the avalanche channel I was tracing, which seemed absolutely to bar further progress. The tried dangers beneath seemed even greater than that of the cliff in front; therefore, after scanning its face again and again, I began to scale it, picking my holds with intense caution. After gaining a point about half-way to the top, I was suddenly brought to a dead stop, with arms outspread, clinging close to the face of the rock, unable to move hand or foot either up or down. My doom appeared fixed. I must fall. There would be a moment of bewilderment, and then a lifeless rumble down the one general precipice to the glacier below.

When this final danger flushed upon me, I became nerve-shaken for the first time since setting foot on the mountains, and my mind seemed to fill with a stifling smoke. But this terrible eclipse lasted only a moment, when life blazed forth again with preternatural clearness. I seemed suddenly to become possessed of a new sense. The other self, bygone experiences, Instinct, or Guardian Angel— call it what you will—came forward and assumed control. . . . The strange influx of strength I had received seemed inexhaustible. I found a way without effort, and soon stood upon the topmost crag in the blessed light.

*"You shall see all things in your heart,*
*and you shall see your heart in me."*

~Krishna

# 30

## Nature as a Poet

No Sierra landscape that I have seen holds anything truly dead or dull, or any trace of what in manufactories is called rubbish or waste; everything is perfectly clean and pure and full of divine lessons. This quick, inevitable interest attaching to everything seems marvelous until the hand of God becomes visible; then it seems reasonable that what interests God may well interest us. When we try to pick out anything by itself, we find it hitched to everything else in the universe. One fancies a heart like our own must be beating in every crystal and cell, and we feel like stopping to speak to the plants and animals as friendly fellow mountaineers. Nature as a poet, an enthusiastic workingman, becomes more and more visible the farther and higher we go; for the mountains are fountains—beginning places, however related to sources beyond mortal ken.

*"The hearth in the home, the altar in the temple,*
*is the hub of the wheel of the earth,*
*the womb of the Universal Mother."*

~Joseph Campbell

# 31

## Sleeping All Our Lives

It is interesting to note among the passengers the play of quickened action in the minds of those who, brought up in the shadows of city business, have been sleeping all their lives. They gaze at the hills of the coast with curious wonder as if never before had they seen a hill. Objects seen every day are scarce seen at all; clocks strike without being heard, as one may even hear the discharge of a cannon so often in the same tone and volume of sound that it is no longer heard. So much need is there for change of scene, new points of view. How many notice so glorious a phenomenon as the rising of the sun over a familiar landscape? All that is necessary to make any landscape visible and therefore impressive is to regard it from a new point of view, or from the old one with our heads upside down. Then we behold a new heaven and earth and are born again, as if we had gone on a pilgrimage to some far-off holy land and had become new creatures with bodies inverted; the scales fall from our eyes, and in like manner are we made to see when we go on excursions into fields and pastures new. . . .

*"O dwellers in the dust, awake and sing for joy!"*
~The Prophet Isaiah

# 32

## Silent Sculptors

The action of flowing ice, whether in the form of river-like glaciers or broad mantles, especially the part it played in sculpturing the earth, is as yet but little understood. Water rivers work openly where people dwell, and so does the rain, and the sea, thundering on all the shores of the world; and the universal ocean of air, though invisible, speaks aloud in a thousand voices, and explains its modes of working and its power. But glaciers, back in their white solitudes, work apart from [people], exerting their tremendous energies in silence and darkness. Outspread, spirit-like, they brood above the predestined landscapes, work on unwearied through immeasurable ages, until, in the fullness of time, the mountains and valleys are brought forth, channels furrowed for rivers, basins made for lakes and meadows, and arms of the sea, soils spread for forests and fields; then they shrink and vanish like summer clouds.

*"We had left no mark on the country itself,*
*but the land had left its mark on us."*

~Sigurd Olson

# 33

## A Leaf in a Whirlwind

[Stickeen] gained the foot of the cliff, while I was on my knees leaning over to give him a lift should he succeed in getting within reach of my arm. Here he halted in dead silence, and it was here I feared he might fail, for dogs are poor climbers. . . . Then suddenly up he came in a springy rush, hooking his paws into the steps and notches so quickly that I could not see how it was done, and whizzed past my head, safe at last!

And now came a scene! "Well done, well done, little boy! Brave boy!" I cried, trying to catch and caress him; but he would not be caught. Never before or since have I seen anything like so passionate a revulsion from the depths of despair to exultant, triumphant, uncontrollable joy. He flashed and darted hither and thither as if fairly demented, screaming and shouting, swirling round and round in giddy loops and cries like a leaf in a whirlwind. . . . When I ran up to him to shake him, fearing he might die of joy, he flashed off two or three hundred yards, his feet in a mist of motion; then, turning suddenly, came back in a wild rush and launched himself at my face, almost knocking me down, all the while screeching and screaming and shouting as if saying, "Saved! saved! saved!"

*"If you touch the leaf deeply enough, it is eternal, deathless."*
~Thich Nhat Hanh

# 34

## How Boundless the Day

How boundless the day seems as we revel in these storm-beaten sky gardens amid so vast a congregation of onlooking mountains! Strange and admirable it is that the more savage and chilly and storm-chafed the mountains, the finer the glow on their faces and the finer the plants they bear. The myriads of flowers tingeing the mountain-top do not seem to have grown out of the dry, rough gravel of disintegration, but rather they appear as visitors, a cloud of witnesses to Nature's love in what we in our timid ignorance and unbelief call howling desert. The surface of the ground, so dull and forbidding at first sight, besides being rich in plants, shines and sparkles with crystals: mica, hornblende, feldspar, quartz, tourmaline.

The radiance in some places is so great as to be fairly dazzling, keen lance rays of every color flashing, sparkling in glorious abundance, joining the plants in their fine, brave beauty-work—every crystal, every flower a window opening into heaven, a mirror reflecting the Creator. . . . Toward sunset, enjoyed a fine run to camp. . .enjoying wild excitement and excess of strength, and so ends a day that will never end.

*"The highest is the inmost or most intimate of all."*
~Hugh of St. Victor

# 35

## Soul Breathe Deep

If you wish to see how much of light, life, and joy can be got into a January, go to this blessed Twenty Hill Hollow. If you wish to see a plant-resurrection, —myriads of bright flowers crowding from the ground, like souls to a judgment—go to Twenty Hills in February. If you are traveling for health, play truant to doctors and friends, fill your pocket with biscuits, and hide in the hills of the Hollow, lave in its waters, tan in its golds, bask in its flower-shine, and your baptisms will make you a new creature indeed. Or, choked in the sediment of society, so tired of the world, here will your hard doubts disappear, your carnal incrustations melt off, and your soul breathe deep and free in God's shoreless atmosphere of beauty and love.

*"The winds of God's grace are always blowing; it is for us to raise our sails."*

~Ramakrishna

# 36

## Sharing the Sky

The groves about the Soda Springs are favorite camping-grounds. . .but there are fine camping-grounds all along the meadows, and one may move from grove to grove every day all summer, enjoying new homes and new beauty to satisfy every roving desire for change.

There are five main capital excursions to be made from here—to the summits of Mounts Dana, Lyell and Coness, and through the Bloody Canyon Pass to Mono Lake and the volcanoes, and down the Tuolumne Canyon, at least as far as the foot of the wonderful series of river cataracts. All of these excursions are sure to be made memorable with joyful health-giving experiences; but perhaps none of them will be remembered with keener delight than the days spent in sauntering on the broad velvet lawns by the river, sharing the sky with the mountains and trees, gaining something of their strength and peace.

*"[Our task is to widen] our circle of compassion to embrace all living beings and all of nature."*
~Albert Einstein

# 37

## Here at the Right Moment

L ook at that, now. Why, it looks as if these giants of God's great army had just now marched into their stations; every one placed just right, just right! What landscape gardening! What a scheme of things! And to think that [God] should plan to bring us feckless creatures here at the right moment, and then flash such glories at us! Man, we're not worthy of such honor!

Praise God from whom all blessings flow!

*"One impulse from a vernal wood, Will teach you more of man,
Of moral evil and of good, Than all the sages can."*

~William Wordsworth

# 38

## Planting Prayers

After witnessing the bad effect of homelessness, developed to so destructive an extent in California, it would assure every lover of their race to see the hearty home-building going on here and the blessed contentment that naturally follows it. Travel-worn pioneers, who have been tossed about like boulders in flood-time, are thronging hither as to a kind of terrestrial heaven, resolved to rest. They build, and plant, and settle, and so come under natural influences. When one plants a tree they plant themselves. Every root is an anchor, over which one rests with grateful interest, and becomes sufficiently calm to feel the joy of living. One necessarily makes the acquaintance of the sun and the sky. Favorite trees fill the mind, and, while tending them like children, and accepting the benefits they bring, one becomes a benefactor. One sees down through the brown common ground teeming with colored fruits, as if it were transparent, and learns to bring them to the surface. What one wills one can raise by true enchantment. With slips and rootlets, magic wands, they appear at the bidding. These, and the seeds they plant, are their prayers, and, by them brought into right relations with God, they work grander miracles every day than ever were written.

*"I think I could stop here myself
and do miracles."*

~Walt Whitman

# 39

## Cat-and-Loon Kin

I carried the wounded loon in my arms; he didn't struggle to get away or offer to strike me, and when I put him on the floor in front of the kitchen stove, he just rested quietly. . . . We had a tortoise-shell cat, an old Tom of great experience who was so fond of lying under the stove in frosty weather. . . he at length advanced a step or two for a nearer view and nearer smell . . . When the beautiful bird, apparently as peaceful and inoffensive as a flower, saw that his hairy yellow enemy had arrived at the right distance, the loon, who evidently was a fine judge of the reach of his spear, shot forward quick as a lightning-flash. . . . Tom was struck right in the centre of his forehead, between the eyes and he bounced straight up in the air like a bucking bronco; and when he alighted after his spring, he rushed madly across the room. . . . Backed against the wall in the farthest corner, he tenderly touched and washed the sore spot, wetting his paw with his tongue, pausing now and then as his courage increased to glare and stare and growl at his enemy with looks and tones wonderfully human, as if saying: "You confounded fishy, unfair rascal! What did you do that for? What had I done to you? Faithless, legless, long-nosed wretch!" Intense experiences like above bring out the humanity that is in all animals. One touch of nature, even a cat-and-loon touch, makes all the world kin.

*"Nature—the Gentlest Mother is."*
~Emily Dickinson

# 40

## Rattling the Instincts

I passed many lovely gardens watered by oozing currentlets, every one of which had lilies in them in the full pomp of bloom, and a rich growth of ferns, chiefly woodwardias and aspidiums and maidenhairs; but toward the base of the mountain the channel was dry, and the chaparral closed over from bank to bank, so that I was compelled to creep more than a mile on hands and knees. In one spot I found an opening in the thorny sky where I could stand erect, and on the further side of the opening discovered a small pool. "Now, here," I said, "I must be careful in creeping, for the birds of the neighborhood come here to drink, and the rattlesnakes come here to catch them." I then began to cast my eye along the channel, perhaps instinctively feeling a snaky atmosphere, and finally discovered one rattler between my feet. But there was a bashful look in his eye, and a withdrawing, deprecating kink in his neck that showed plainly as words could tell that he would not strike, and only wished to be let alone. I therefore passed on, lifting my foot a little higher than usual, and left him to enjoy his life in this his own home.

*"I was up to my knees in the world."*
~Annie Dillard

# 41
## The Animal Within

Surely a better time must be drawing nigh when godlike human beings will become truly humane, and learn to put their animal fellow mortals in their hearts instead of on their backs or in their dinners. In the mean time we may just as well as not learn to live clean, innocent lives instead of slimy, bloody ones. All hale, red-blooded boys are savage, the best and boldest the savagest, fond of hunting and fishing. But when thoughtless childhood is past, the best rise the highest above all this bloody flesh and sport business, the wild foundational animal dying out day by day, as divine uplifting, transfiguring charity grows in. . . .

And surely all God's people, however serious and savage, great or small, like to play.

*"She changed Herself into the forms of various animals."*
~The Great-Forest Upanishad

# 42

## You Ought To Have Been With Me

Ah! I'm glad to be in camp. The glacier almost got me this time. If it had not been for the beacon and old Towaatt, I might have had to spend the night on the ice. The crevasses were so many and so bewildering in their mazy, crisscross windings that I was actually going farther into the glacier when I caught the flash of light. . . .

Man, man; you ought to have been with me. You'll never make up what you have lost to-day. I've been wandering through a thousand rooms of God's crystal temple. I've been a thousand feet down in the crevasses, with matchless domes and sculptured figures and carved ice-work all about me. Solomon's marble and ivory palaces were nothing to it. Such purity, such color, such delicate beauty! I was tempted to stay there and feast my soul, and softly freeze, until I would become part of the glacier. What a great death that would be!

*"Thus the Unspeakable used to speak to Moses face to face, as one speaks to a friend."*

~The Torah

# 43

## Campfire

Slight rain-storms are likely to be encountered in a trip round the mountain, but one may easily find shelter beneath well-thatched trees that shed the rain like a roof. Then the shining of the wet leaves is delightful, and the steamy fragrance, and the burst of bird-song from a multitude of thrushes and finches and warblers that have nests in the chaparral. The nights, too, are delightful, watching with Shasta beneath the great starry dome. A thousand thousand voices are heard, but so finely blended they seem a part of the night itself, and make a deeper silence. And how grandly do the great logs and branches of your campfire give forth the heat and light that during their long century-lives they have so slowly gathered from the sun, storing it away in beautiful dotted cells and beads of amber gum! The neighboring trees look into the charmed circle as if the noon of another day had come, familiar flowers and grasses that chance to be near seem far more beautiful and impressive than by day, and as the dead trees give forth their light all the other riches of their lives seem to be set free and with the rejoicing flames rise again to the sky.

*"This world was and is and shall be ever-living Fire."*
~Heraclitus

# 44

## River!

The canyon begins near the lower end of the meadows and extends to the Hetch Hetchy Valley, a distance of about eighteen miles, though it will seem much longer to any one who scrambles through it. It is from twelve hundred to about five thousand feet deep. . . . The sheer falls, except when the snow is melting in early spring, are quite small in volume as compared with those of Yosemite and Hetch Hetchy; though in any other country many of them would be regarded as wonders. But it is the cascades or sloping falls on the main river that are the crowning glory of the canyon, and these in volume, extent and variety surpass those of any other canyon in the Sierra. . . . For miles the river is one wild, exulting, on-rushing mass of snowy purple bloom spreading over glacial waves of granite without any definite channel, gliding in magnificent silver plumes, dashing and foaming through huge boulder-dams, leaping high into the air in wheel-like whirls, displaying glorious enthusiasm, tossing from side to side, doubling, glinting, singing in exuberance of mountain energy.

*"[The Tree speaks]: Come to me, here beside the River.*
*Plant yourself beside the River."*

~Maya Angelou

# 45

## Traveling the Milky Way

We all travel the milky way together, trees and people; but it never occurred to me until this storm-day, while swinging in the wind, that trees are travelers, in the ordinary sense. They make many journeys, not extensive ones, it is true; but our own little journeys, away and back again, are only little more than tree-wavings—many of them not so much. When the storm began to abate, I dismounted and sauntered down through the calming woods. The storm-tones died away, and, turning toward the east, I beheld the countless hosts of the forests hushed and tranquil, towering above one another on the slopes of the hills like a devout audience. The setting sun filled them with amber light, and seemed to say, while they listened, "My peace I give unto you."

"To see a World in a Grain of Sand,
and a Heaven in a Wild Flower."

~William Blake

# 46

## Summit

At length, after gaining the upper extreme of our guiding ridge, we found a good place to rest and prepare ourselves to scale the dangerous upper curves of the dome. . . .Thus prepared, we stepped forth afresh, slowly groping our way through tangled lines of crevasses, crossing on snow bridges here and there after cautiously testing them, jumping at narrow places, or crawling around the ends of the largest, bracing well at every point with our alpenstocks and setting our spiked shoes squarely down on the dangerous slopes. It was nerve-trying work, most of it, but we made good speed nevertheless, and by noon all stood together on the utmost summit. . . . We remained on the summit nearly two hours, looking about us at the vast maplike views [that] could hardly be surpassed in sublimity and grandeur; but one feels far from home so high in the sky, so much so that one is inclined to guess that, apart from the acquisition of knowledge and the exhilaration of climbing, more pleasure is to be found at the foot of mountains than on their frozen tops. Doubly happy, however, is the person to whom lofty mountain-tops are within reach, for the lights that shine there illumine all that lies below.

*"O the mind, mind has mountains."*
~Gerard Manley Hopkins

# 47

## Alma Mater

Although I was four years at the University, I did not take the regular course of studies, but instead picked out what I thought would be most useful to me, particularly chemistry, which opened a new world, and mathematics and physics, a little Greek and Latin, botany and geology. I was far from satisfied with what I had learned, and should have stayed longer. Anyhow I wandered away on a glorious botanical and geological excursion, which has lasted nearly fifty years and is not yet completed, always happy and free, poor and rich, without thought of a diploma or of making a name, urged on and on through endless, inspiring, Godful beauty.

From the top of a hill on the north side of Lake Mendota I gained a last wistful, lingering view of the beautiful University grounds and buildings where I had spent so many hungry and happy and hopeful days. There with streaming eyes I bade my blessed Alma Mater farewell. But I was only leaving one University for another, the Wisconsin University for the University of the Wilderness.

"How could I resist my nature,
That lives for oneness with God?"

~Mechthild

# 48

## Writing History

We are going to write some history. Think of the honor! We have been chosen to put some interesting people and some of Nature's grandest scenes on the page of human record and on the map. Hurry! We are daily losing the most important news of all the world.

Ah! What a Lord's mercy it is that we lost this glacier last fall, when we were pressed for time, to find it again in these glorious days that have flashed out of the mists for our special delectation. This has been a day of days. I have found four new varieties of moss, and have learned many new and wonderful facts about world-shaping. And then, the wonder and glory! Why, all the values of beauty and sublimity—form, color, motion and sound—have been present to-day at their very best. My friend, we are the richest people in all the world to-night.

*"Our every act has a universal dimension."*
~The Dalai Lama

# 49

## Wherever You Go,
## I Will Be With You

When a special messenger was sent [by Major Savage] to the chief he appeared the next day. He came entirely alone and stood in dignified silence before one of the guards until invited to enter the camp. He was recognized as Tenaya, the old chief of the Grizzly Bear Tribe. [He said]:

*My people, do not want anything from the Great Father you tell me about. The Great Spirit is our father and he has always supplied us with all we need. We do not want anything from white people. Our women are able to do our work. Go, then. Let us remain in the mountains where we were born, where the ashes of our fathers have been given to the wind. . . .*

*You may kill me, Sir Captain, but you shall not live in peace. I will follow in your footsteps. I will not leave my home, but be with the spirits among the rocks, the waterfalls, in the rivers and in the winds; wherever you go I will be with you. You will not see me but you will fear the spirit of the old chief and grow cold. The Great Spirit has spoken. I am done.*

This expedition finally captured the remnants of the tribes at the head of Lake Tenaya and took them to the Fresno reservation, together with their chief, Tenaya.

*"We call upon all those who have lived upon this earth
to teach us, and show us the Way."*

~Chinook blessing

# 50

## Keep Close to Nature's Heart

You are going on a strange journey this time, my friend. I don't envy you. You'll have a hard time keeping your heart light and simple in the midst of this crowd of madmen. Instead of the music of the wind among the spruce-tops and the tinkling of the waterfalls, your ears will be filled with the oaths and groans of these poor, deluded, self-burdened people. Keep close to Nature's heart, yourself; and break clear away, once in a while, and climb a mountain or spend a week in the woods. Wash your spirit clean from the earth-stains of this sordid, gold-seeking crowd in God's pure air. It will help you in your efforts to bring to these people something better than gold. Don't lose your freedom and your love of the Earth as God made it.

*"The Energy that holds up mountains
is the energy I bow down to."*

~Mirabai

# 51

## Scootchers & Profships

How much I enjoyed this excursion, or indeed any excursion in the wilderness, I am not able to tell. I must have been born a mountaineer and the climbs and "scootchers" of boyhood days about the old Dunbar Castle and on the roof of our house made fair beginnings. I suppose old age will put an end to scrambling in rocks and ice, but I can still climb as well as ever.

Then came Emerson and more preaching. He said, "Don't tarry too long in the woods. Listen for the word of your guardian angel. You are needed by the young people in our colleges. Solitude is a sublime mistress, but an intolerable wife. When Heaven gives the sign, leave the mountains. . . ."

Then came Asa Gray and more fine rambles and sermons. He said, "When you get ready, come to Harvard. . . ."

But you must surely know that I never for a moment thought of leaving God's big show for a mere profship, call who may.

"Within is the fountain of good, and it will ever bubble up,
if thou wilt ever dig."
~Marcus Aurelius

# 52

## From the Gardens of the Poor

Everybody needs beauty as well as bread, places to play in and pray in, where Nature may heal and cheer and give strength to body and soul alike. This natural beauty-hunger is made manifest in the little window-sill gardens of the poor, though perhaps only a geranium slip in a broken cup, as well as in the carefully tended rose and lily gardens of the rich, the thousands of spacious city parks and botanical gardens, and in our magnificent National parks. . . .

These temple destroyers, devotees of ravaging commercialism, seem to have a perfect contempt for Nature, and, instead of lifting their eyes to the God of the mountains, lift them to the Almighty Dollar.

Dam Hetch Hetchy! As well dam for water-tanks the people's cathedrals and churches, for no holier temple has ever been consecrated by the heart. . . .

*"Naething comes fairer to licht
than what has been lang hidden."*

~Scottish proverb

# 53

## Child of the Wilderness

Though he was apparently as cold as a glacier and about as impervious to fun, I tried hard to make his acquaintance, guessing there must be something worth while hidden beneath so much courage, endurance, and love of wild-weathery adventure. . . .

Like children, most small dogs beg to be loved and allowed to love; but Stickeen seemed a very Diogenes, asking only to be let alone: a true child of the wilderness, holding the even tenor of his hidden life with the silence and serenity of nature. His strength of character lay in his eyes. They looked as old as the hills, and as young, and as wild. I never tired of looking into them: it was like looking into a landscape. . . .

I was accustomed to look into the faces of plants and animals, and I watched the little sphinx more and more keenly as an interesting study. But there is no estimating the wit and wisdom concealed and latent in our lower fellow mortals until made manifest by profound experiences; for it is through suffering that dogs as well as saints are developed and made perfect.

*"I am looking for one honest person."*
~Diogenes (the "dog philosopher")

# 54

## Yosemite Kirk

I am sitting here in a little shanty made of sugar pine shingles this Sabbath evening. I have not been at church a single time since leaving home. Yet this glorious valley might well be called a church, for every lover of the great Creator who comes within the broad overwhelming influences of the place fails not to worship as they never did before. The glory of the Lord is upon all God's works; it is written plainly upon all the fields of every clime, and upon every sky, but here in this place of surpassing glory the Lord has written in capitals. I hope that one day you will see and read with your own eyes.

The only sounds that strike me tonight are the ticking of the clock, the flickering of the fire and the love songs of a host of peaceful frogs that sing out in the meadow up to their throats in slush, and the deep waving roar of the falls like breakers on a rocky coast. . . . I have completed the sawmill here. It works extremely well. If not a "Kirk and a mill" I have at least made a house and a mill here.

*"My heart's in the Highlands wherever I go."*
~Robert Burns

# 55

## Circle of Friends

To lovers of the wild, these mountains are not a hundred miles away. Their spiritual power and the goodness of the sky make them near, as a circle of friends.

You cannot feel yourself out of doors; plain, sky, and mountains ray beauty which you feel. You bathe in these spirit-beams, turning round and round, as if warming at a camp-fire. Presently you lose consciousness of your own separate existence: you blend with the landscape, and become part and parcel of nature.

"*The Bodhisattva practices great friendliness.*"
~Siddhartha Gautama, the Buddha

# 56

## Come Higher

Ramble to the summit of Mount Hoffman, eleven thousand feet high, the highest point in life's journey my feet have yet touched. And what glorious landscapes are about me, new plants, new animals, new crystals, and multitudes of new mountains far higher than Hoffman, towering in glorious array along the axis of the range, serene, majestic, snow-laden, sun-drenched, vast domes and ridges shining below them, forests, lakes, and meadows in the hollows, the pure blue bell-flower sky brooding them all—a glory day of admission into a new realm of wonders as if Nature had wooingly whispered, "Come higher." What questions I asked, and how little I know of all the vast show, and how eagerly, tremulously hopeful of some day knowing more, learning the meaning of these divine symbols crowded together on this wondrous page.

*"I go and come with a strange liberty in Nature,
a part of herself."*

~Henry Thoreau

# 57

## Wild Tricks

Of course I am anxious to see as much of the
wilderness as possible in the few days left me,
and I say again—May the good time come when I
can stay as long as I like with plenty of bread, far
and free from trampling flocks, though I may well be
thankful for this generous foodful inspiring summer.
Anyhow we never know where we must go nor what
guides we are to get—[people], storms, guardian
angels, or sheep. Perhaps almost everybody in the
least natural is guarded more than [they] are ever
aware of. All the wilderness seems to be full of tricks
and plans to drive and draw us up into God's Light.

*"Perhaps humankind, in the middle of its path. . .is nearer to its
actual goal than it will be at the end."*

~Friedrich Nietzsche

# 58

## Waiting To Be Blessed

Climbing along the dashing border of the cascade, bathed from time to time in waftings of irised spray, you are not likely to feel much weariness, and all too soon you find yourself beyond its highest fountains. Climbing higher, new beauty comes streaming on the sight. . . .

All the streams and the pools at this elevation are furnished with little gardens, which, though making scarce any show at a distance, constitute charming surprises to the appreciative mountaineer in their midst. In so wild and so beautiful a region your first day will be spent, every sight and sound novel and inspiring, and leading you far from yourself. . . .

With the approach of evening long, blue, spiky-edged shadows creep out over the snowfields, while a rosy glow, at first scarce discernible, gradually deepens, suffusing every peak and flushing the glaciers and the harsh crags above them. This is the alpenglow, the most impressive of all the terrestrial manifestations of God. At the touch of this divine light the mountains seem to kindle to a rapt religious consciousness, and stand hushed like worshippers waiting to be blessed. Then suddenly comes darkness and the stars.

*"In the silence of the woods, you will not be alone."*
~Chief Sealth

# 59

## Come to the Woods,
## for Here Is Rest

Come to the woods, for here is rest.
There is no repose like that of the
green deep woods.
Here grow the wallflower and the violet.
The squirrel will come and sit upon your knee,
the logcock will wake you in the morning.
Sleep in forgetfulness of all ill.
Of all the upness accessible to mortals,
there is no upness comparable to the mountains.

*"I am restored in beauty. I am restored in beauty.
I am restored in beauty."*

~Navajo prayer

# 60

## All the World Seems a Church

No feature, however, of all the noble landscape as seen from here seems more wonderful than the Cathedral itself, a temple displaying Nature's best masonry and sermons in stone. How often I have gazed at it from the tops of hills and ridges, and through openings in the forests on my many short excursions, devoutly wondering, admiring, longing! This I may say is the first time I have been at church in California, led here at last, every door graciously opened for the poor lonely worshipper. In our best times everything turns into religion, all the world seems a church and the mountains altars. And lo, here at last in front of the Cathedral is blessed cassiope, ringing her thousands of sweet-toned bells, the sweetest church music I ever enjoyed. Listening, admiring, until late in the afternoon I compelled myself to hasten away. . . .

*"—these are the music and pictures of
the most ancient religion."*

~Ralph Waldo Emerson

# Sources

In the preceding text the source of each Muir quote is identified by a particular leaf icon, shown following the passage. Below is a key to those sources:

*Alaska Days with John Muir*
> Samuel Hall Young, ed. Fleming H. Revell Co., New York: 1915.

*The Cruise of the Corwin*
> William Frederic Badè, ed. Houghton Mifflin Company, The Riverside Press Cambridge, Boston and New York: 1917.

*John of the Mountains:*
*The Unpublished Journals of John Muir*
> Linne Marsh Wolfe, ed. Houghton Mifflin Company: 1938 by Wanda Muir Hanna, renewed 1966 by John Muir Hanna and Ralph Eugene Wolfe.

*John Muir: His Life and Letters*
*and Other Writings*
> Terry Gifford, ed. The Mountaineers, Seattle, Washington: 1996.

*The Mountains of California*
> The Century Co., New York: 1894.

*My First Summer in the Sierra*
> Houghton Mifflin Company, The Riverside Press Cambridge, Boston and New York: 1911.

*Our National Parks*
> Houghton Mifflin Company, The Riverside Press Cambridge, Boston and New York: 1901.

*Steep Trails*
> Essay originally written in 1875. William Frederic Badè, ed., Berkeley, California: 1918.

*The Story of My Boyhood and Youth*
> Houghton Mifflin Company, The Riverside Press Cambridge, Boston and New York, 1912.

*A Thousand-Mile Walk to the Gulf*
> William Frederic Badè, ed. Houghton Mifflin Company, The Riverside Press Cambridge, Boston and New York: 1916.

*Travels in Alaska*
> Houghton Mifflin Company, The Riverside Press Cambridge, Boston and New York: 1915.

*The Yosemite*
> The Century Co., New York: 1912.

# Acknowledgments

Permission to reprint copyright or manuscript material has been gratefully received from the following:

Houghton Mifflin Company, for portions of *John of the Mountains*, edited by Linnie Marsh Wolfe (copyright 1938 by Wanda Muir Hanna and 1966 by John Muir Hanna and Ralph Eugene Wolfe); and *The Life and Letters of John Muir*, by W.F. Badè (copyright 1924; renewed in 1951 by John Muir Hanna).

# Photos

All photos by Chris Highland.

# Highland Companion

The one with muddy boots and sap on his hands,
with pantlegs soaked in the baptism of waterfall
spray, is CHRIS HIGHLAND. He is a minister, a chaplain,
a spiritual scootcher who has led expeditions into
wisdom traditions, along mystic trails and heretic
paths, for many a year.

A graduate of Seattle Pacific University with a
degree in Religion and Philosophy, Chris came to
Marin County, California to earn his Masters at San
Francisco Theological Seminary in San Anselmo. His
long journey as a chaplain has taken him from
schools to jails to the streets, and his adventure of
the heart has led him from the Cascades to the
Sierras to the Rockies, and to the Highlands of
Scotland.

Originally from Seattle, Washington, Chris lives
in San Rafael, California—just a gentle saunter from
the redwood-filled hollows, jagged bluffs and white
dashing water described by Muir as he steamed into
and out the Golden Gateway toward his beloved
temples.

By the same author: *The Homeless God.*